Playing Soccer

An ARM CHAIR GUIDE

Full of 100 Tips to Getting Better at Soccer

Arm Chair Guides

Playing Soccer:
An Arm Chair Guide Full of 100 Tips to Getting Better at Soccer

Published by
Arm Chair Guides

Printed in the United States of America

ISBN-13: 978-0615502083
ISBN-10: 0615502083

Visit the Arm Chair Guides site at:
www.ArmChairGuides.com/PlayingSoccer

Overview

Soccer has evolved through the centuries into a sport that requires many skills. A good soccer player will not just focus on one area.

Being a good kicker doesn't make you a good player. You must have skills in passing and receiving as well for the coach to feel safe putting you in the game.

Young soccer players can develop their skills and see their game improve by focusing on some fundamental ideas.

Using these basic ideas in your training sessions will help you become a well-rounded player with a variety of skills, regardless of position.

Dribble at the right place and the right time.

Dribbling can be used in your opponent's 18 yard box to create some mystery concerning what your next move will be. It should never be done in your own half of the field or just to draw attention to yourself. It is important to know when to use dribbling, and when it's better just to pass the ball to another teammate.

Be confident.

Your best soccer skills are only as good as your confidence in using them. When faced with a difficult situation, relax and carefully determine your next move. Whether you are dribbling or receiving the ball, exuding confidence will help you become a successful player.

Use your weak foot.

Using your weak foot is important to your dribbling success. It may be frustrating, but changing feet can help your team keep the ball. Your opponent will defend your strong side, so switching to your weak foot can catch him by surprise and throw him off.

It's about balance and rhythm.

When dribbling, it is important to move with rhythm and balance. Your movements while dribbling the ball allow you to get past your opponent and closer to the goal. Be ready to move quickly in any direction by staying on the balls of your feet. By doing this, you may catch your opponent off guard and get past him.

Know your opponent's weak side.

Most players tend to favor a particular side; therefore, they are stronger on that side. If a player is right-handed, they may be weaker on their left side and vice versa. If you can determine their weaker side, it may be to your advantage. Be aware though that many players are skilled in using both sides, so this advice may not always work.

Practice the Ronaldhino dribble.

Ronaldinho's snake move, also called the *elastico* or flip-flap, is done in one swift motion. Move the ball from the outside of the foot, then flip it back with the inside of the foot. This move can be done by standing on your left foot, and flipping it with the right foot.

Try the lunge.

The dummy step-over involves getting your foot in front of the ball to the outside. You fake your opponent out by lunging with the left foot, then taking the ball toward the right with the outside of your foot. Move your shoulders toward the side you are faking so that your defender will fall for your trick.

Use the double lunge.

This move involves a skating motion that can fake out your opponent. You have to lunge with your left foot toward the left, then with your right foot toward the right. Now that your opponent is wondering what your next move will be, you steal the ball away with the outside of your left foot.

Learn the Puskas move.

Named after one of the greatest footballers, this move involves a fake as you shoot the ball and resembles a V-shape on the ground. Move the ball diagonally across your body and act like you're going to shoot the ball with the top of your foot. You then pull the ball back and push it outside with the inside of your foot. This dribbling move is effective when your opponent is really close to you.

Improve your free kick ability.

Free kicks involve putting your non-kicking foot next to the ball, even to the center of the ball. This allows for better accuracy as you kick. You are then ready to swing your kicking leg into motion and get ready to strike.

Hit the ball with your heads and shoulders down.

The position of your body in relation to the ball is important for success in soccer. Make sure your shoulders are square over the ball and that your body is straight. Don't lean your head back when you kick. Keeping your head and shoulders down during contact will allow for optimal strength in your legs.

Kick with your laces.

Develop your kicking technique by kicking the ball with the top of your foot instead of your toes. The top of your foot is shaped so that it cradles the ball which gives you much more control over the ball. Hit it on the top of your shoelaces with your toes pointing downward.

Pay attention to the follow-through.

If your foot meets the ball at the appropriate spot, follow through is a natural motion. Follow the kick all the way through to ensure maximum force on the ball. Work on techniques which add movement to the ball. Many professional players add spin to the ball which creates more confusion for goalies.

Stop the shot.

For goalkeepers, the best way to stop a shot is to put your entire body behind the ball. If you can't get your whole body behind the ball, get as much of it as possible. Get two hands or legs instead of one, and in some cases maybe the slightest touch of a fingertip can change the course of the ball.

Drop to your knees and grab the ball.

Shots along the ground are some of the most difficult for the goalkeeper to block. The safest way to block these shots is to drop to your knees and grab the ball with both hands. If you're flexible enough, you may choose to bend your back and stoop over to get the ball.

Get down low quickly.

It is important to get down low as quickly as possible in order to save the ball. Many shots land between your knee and waist and require using your chest as a scoop to get control over the ball. It is natural for your body to fall forward, cupping the ball safely to your chest.

Take it into your chest.

There are two techniques for catching the ball at chest level. You can allow the ball to impact your body, and cup your hands around it as it hits. Be careful not to let the ball bounce off your chest into your opponent's hands. Also, you may choose to bring your hands out in front of you and catch the ball with your fingers spread open.

Try to stop every shot.

Always make an attempt to block the ball. Often you may surprise yourself by actually stopping seemingly impossible shots. Your teammates will cheer you on and understand if you miss. If you hit the ground, jump back up quickly and get ready. If you are injured, recover quickly and deal with your injuries later, if possible.

Focus.

Concentration is the key for goalkeepers to keep the ball out of the net. Keep constant communication with your team even if you are not involved in the particular play. Focus on the play, cheer them on, give them directions, and stay ready for the ball.

20

Try to anticipate the play before it happens.

Stay two steps ahead of the other team by reading their body language and guessing their next moves. This will allow you to be ready to stop the ball before it hits the net.

Try punching the ball with your fists.

There are some instances where it is not possible to catch the ball and throw it to your teammate. If this happens, try punching the ball with your fists before it hits the net. Punching the ball as far away as possible allows your teammates to try to regain control of the ball again.

Slow down.

As goalkeeper, it is your job to determine the speed of the game. If it would benefit your team to slow the pace down, take your time to distribute the ball to your teammates. For faster pace plays, punt the ball quickly out into the field.

Never use the top of your head to hit the ball.

If using your head to make a play, always use your forehead. Your forehead is optimal because it is thicker and flat, and allows for more control of the ball. You can see the ball up until it makes contact, therefore allowing for more accuracy and control. Using your forehead will also be painless compared to using the top of you head.

Eye on the ball.

Try to avoid the natural instinct to close your eyes when something is coming straight at your head. Even the professionals sometimes close their eyes during these plays, but it is always better to keep them open as long as possible. This will give you more awareness of how fast the ball is coming and accuracy when it leaves your head.

Attack the ball.

When the ball comes your way, don't just let it hit you, but try to attack the ball. Move forward to meet the ball, and for maximum power, arch your back and knob your head forward during contact. Using your neck muscles during contact can also add power to your play.

Want to learn all these tips while actually doing them?

Visit
www.ArmChairGuides.com/PlayingSoccer

Sign up and download
your AUDIO COPY
of **Playing Soccer: An Arm Chair Guide Full of 100 Tips
to Getting Better at Soccer**
for FREE.

Need to multitask?
Need to relax your strained eyes after work?
Need to do your laundry?

Pick up some valuable advice to get you started and integrate it into your lifestyle. Since the tips are being read aloud, you'll no longer have a reason not to start playing soccer.

Practice juggling.

Juggling is a skill that takes lots of practice. Start with a feet-to-hand motion, dropping the ball from your hands to your feet, then kicking it back up to your hands. Work on keeping this motion going for several rounds, eventually adding in a foot switch. The more you practice, the more you will learn to control the ball, and use your body surfaces to move the ball around.

27

Learn how to juggle by going in a cycle.

When learning to juggle, go in a cycle from your feet to your thighs to your head and back. The important thing is that you are in control of the ball, and not just struggling to keep it in the air. You can then begin to try more complicated moves such as faking out your opponent by kicking the ball slightly to the right, then moving it left. You can also try walking or jogging while juggling the ball across the field.

Learn to control the ball.

There are many good reasons for learning to juggle. The most important is learning to control the ball and use all the surfaces of your feet. This can be a life saver during a game. You might be surprised at the different moves you can make using your feet that might just save the game or get your ball to the goal!

29

Strengthen your weaker leg.

Wall ball juggling involves knocking the ball against a wall with your foot. Try switching from the outside to the inside of your foot so that you are prepared to make a pass or shoot the ball. Try to keep the ball going without letting it bounce more than once, varying the power each time. This is a great workout that will challenge any player, and help build strength in those weaker leg muscles.

Go up and down.

Practice juggling the ball up and down using every surface of your body. Start by juggling in a certain order such as foot, thigh, head, thigh, foot, etc. Once you become comfortable with the order, make yourself be more specific such as left foot, right thigh, etc. You can also add in shoulder, between thighs, and head juggles for more difficulty.

Learn the 'around the world' trick.

The 'around the world' move is performed by circling your foot around the ball. When the ball hits the area between your thigh and shoulder, use your right foot to circle the ball over and back under, then continue juggling the ball. Try the same move using your left foot.

Enhance your passing skills.

There are two types of passes that players must become confident at: short and long. For shorter passes, your feet should be facing your target directly beside the ball. Kick the center of the ball with the largest part of your foot, and follow through the kick for maximum power. For a longer pass, the ball should be kicked with toes down using the laces area of the foot. Be sure to hit the ball firmly, so that the ball does not slow down before it reaches its target.

Determine the right pass.

The type of pass you use is determined by defensive pressure and field position. If you are passing to someone who is under defensive pressure, pass to the side where the defender is not positioned. If a player is leading a pass to the goal, you can pass the ball directly in front of him. This saves the player valuable time which could lead to a goal.

Think on your feet.

A successful soccer team is one that can think quickly and make decisions about passing the ball. You must identify open players, and get the ball to open areas of the field for play. Pass the ball to areas where the defense is thin. Players that get out of position can run to an open area and accept the pass.

Practice receiving the ball using the inside of your foot.

You can practice by kicking the ball against a wall and receiving it inside. This technique is quite easy to learn, but takes lots of practice.

Use the instep.

The instep is a part of the body that can be used when there is not much defensive pressure from the opposing team. This is also an effective technique when using a slide tackle to steal back the ball from your opponent.

Receive with your thigh.

The thigh is a common part of the body used for keeping the ball on the move. This body part can be used when the opposition is closing in on you. The area just below the shorts will give you control over the ball.

Learn to receive the ball using your chest.

The chest is a large surface for bouncing off the ball. The best strategy for this move is practicing until you are accustomed to the ball hitting your chest, which can be painful at first. This move can be used to control the ball when there are opponents around you.

Shield the ball.

Shielding the ball from your opponent is best done using your body. You can practice this by trying to dribble the ball in a small space. Protect the ball with your body and fight for the ball with intensity.

Carry the ball to the open space.

Carrying the ball to open space can prevent the opposing team from getting the ball. Carry the ball with inside of your foot, dragging the ball to the open space. It is important to make sure your opponent does not steal the ball by bending your knees and shielding the ball from him. Shield the ball by cutting the ball between the inside and outside of your foot. You will eventually find yourself using both feet to shield the ball.

Switch directions.

Keep them guessing by switching the direction of the ball as you pass it back and forth between your feet. Use all the parts of your foot to keep your opponent off guard. Occasionally turn and take on your opponent.

Anticipate the defender's moves.

One of the keys to overcoming a defender while shielding is to anticipate his moves. If the defender moves in one direction, keep the ball moving in the opposite direction. Once way to anticipate their moves is to touch them with your body and arm. You can also push against them to keep them away.

Be aggressive.

You must be aggressive to keep you opponent at bay. You should push against him before it's too late. Build your upper body strength so that you can overcome him when he pushes. If you feel that you are being overtaken, take other actions such as diving to keep from losing the ball.

Shoot with accuracy.

Shooting the ball requires you to be in position on top of the ball in order to make the shot with accuracy. You can touch the ball using the inside, outside, and laces of the foot, depending on your position. Make sure your opponent is not close, so that the shot is not blocked.

Know where the goalie is.

If possible, look up at the goalie before you shoot. This allows the shooter to know where to kick the ball and hit the net. Often though, there is no time for this before the shot.

46

Take a look at the ball before shooting.

When shooting the ball, it is important to look at it first. With all of the commotion on the field, players tend to look at their defenders instead of looking at the ball. Taking a second to look at the ball can often mean the difference between hitting their target and losing the ball.

47

Position your non-kicking foot.

The non-kicking foot must be in position before you kick. Do a little hop to get your foot into position so that you have more power in the shot. There are four types of positions depending on where you want the ball to go. Your stance should never be too wide or your feet too far from the ball; otherwise, you may miss the goal.

Put more power in your kick.

Your shooting leg should come back as far as possible when kicking. The legs will assume a v-shape, and the farther back you can go, the more power you will gain in your kick. So if you're having trouble kicking, notice how far you bring your kicking leg back during a shot.

Contain an attacker should be done from an angle.

Containing an attacker should be done from an angle, and never from a head on position. Bend your knees and lean forward so that you maintain stability. Move with your opponent and force him toward the sideline if necessary.

Stop your opponent.

A block tackle is a way to stop your opponent and force him to give up the ball. In order to do this, your supporting foot must be firmly planted on the ground; while your free foot goes in the direction he is moving. Ideally this will cause him to stumble, while maintaining your position.

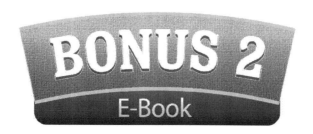

BONUS 2

E-Book

Bring these tips anywhere you go—
on the bus, train or while standing in line!

Head to
www.ArmChairGuides.com/PlayingSoccer

Sign up and grab
the **Playing Soccer: An Arm Chair Guide Full of 100 Tips
to Getting Better at Soccer**
E-BOOK BUNDLE (in PDF, ePub and Mobi) for FREE.

Do you want to read your Arm Chair Guides book on your
device? Do you want to adjust the font size and still be
able to add notes and bookmarks or highlight the text?

Download the free e-book bundle, which comes in 3
popular formats, and view them using your favorite
reader. Learn some valuable tips to prepare for the game
anytime, anywhere.

Tackle the ball.

Poke tackling is a move that can be used to gain control of the ball. You use your foot to reach out and stab the ball, loosening your opponent's grasp on the ball. Slide tackling can be used for opponents on the sideline or shielding the ball.

Decrease the offensive threat.

Jostling your opponent involves using your shoulder to gain possession of the ball or at least get him off course. Just be careful not to get carried away and get a foul in the process of jostling the player.

Get between the goal and the ball.

Surprise attacks can often cause your opponent to give up the ball. A forward lunge involves sneaking up on your opponent from behind, and lunging at him from the front. The point of this move is to wedge yourself between your opponent and the ball, therefore gaining control of the ball.

Confuse the other team.

There are several throw-in techniques which require your teammates to react to the ball. The crossover involves two players close to the throw-in spot, switching places, confusing the opponent. This move might just be enough to confuse the other team and gain possession of the ball.

Use the trick throw-in.

The trick throw-in is actually a trick that will throw your opponent off and hopefully catch him by surprise. In this play, the thrower fakes a discussion with a teammate. As the teammate walks away, he throws the ball into his back. This trick is sometimes effective for gaining control of the ball.

Get a crosser take the throw.

If you're team is having difficulty getting throw-ins to the penalty box, consider a crosser. The crosser can take the ball to a teammate who can one-touch the ball back to the thrower. This allows the thrower to get the ball into the penalty box with one touch.

Have the player closest to the ball take the throw.

In a sticky situation, the player closest to the ball should take the throw. This goes against the idea that only the left and right backs should take throw-ins, and in positional attacks, this is better. But if the situation calls for a quick throw, the player closer to the ball is the best man for the job.

Boost your throw-in skills.

There are three techniques for successful throw-ins. First of all, build your upper body strength and work on your actual throwing techniques. There are many great soccer players whose techniques and body movement should be studied. Also, communicate with you teammates and develop a throwing technique that will keep your opponents guessing.

Set up a corner kick.

Corner kicks are a delivery technique in which right footers can come from the left and vice versa. If the ball is not coming from the proper trajectory, the opposing team may need runners to meet the ball in case the target is missed. The kicker can hold up his hand and lower it when he takes the kick to help his team get ready for the play.

Have 5 or 6 runners in the penalty area when taking a corner kick.

Near-post runners can be sent in to head on the goal, or get the ball to players near the goal who can judge the ball's flight and get it into the goal. Back-post runners can watch for any long crosses and for the opportunity to head the ball into the goal.

Defend corner kicks.

In youth soccer leagues, man-to-man defending is simpler and recommended. Once you get into the professional games, zone-to-zone defending is more common. It requires players to keep open and effective communication between them and the goalkeeper who can keep an eye open for open attackers.

Use a common corner kick strategy.

Most coaches often put a defender on each goal post for keeping shots clear off the line. This helps prevent close kicks from coming in, and once the kick is intercepted, those defenders may move out to defend attackers who may be left open.

Take charge.

The goalkeeper has many jobs; one of those can be defending corner kicks. He must ensure all runners are accounted for, and make sure they are covered. When a corner is allowed, the goalkeeper must communicate with his teammates and let them know how he intends to defend the ball. Catching the ball is best, and if possession is taken, breaking quickly is necessary to avoid opposition.

64

Train for running both with and without the ball.

Running with the ball is something that takes practice, but speed can save the game. It may not seem natural, but keep the ball close to you and touch it with every step.

Work out and improve your physical core.

If you have strength in your legs, abs, chest, shoulders, backs, and arms, you will see an overall increase in speed. Practice is the key, and working on your technique and strength is the only way to improve your speed.

Be competitive.

Playing soccer requires a competitive attitude. You can work on this by racing a friend or family member who naturally brings out that competitive spirit in you. The more you desire to win, the more you will put into the race, and find out just how fast you can really go.

Sprint uphill.

The key to running fast is building muscles, especially leg muscles. Try sprinting uphill for maximum resistance in your legs. They will be sore and hurt afterwards, but your leg muscles will get stronger, and your speed will increase with these workouts.

Train with a parachute.

Another way to increase resistance during workouts is to attach a parachute to your back. When you run, the wind catches the parachutes, and resistance increases. After you train with parachutes for a while, you can take them off and still remember the proper running techniques.

Try to relax.

Tension is an important factor to consider when training for speed. If your joints and muscles are tense or tight, it will prevent you from running at your maximum speed. Try to relax and do some stretches to warm up so that your muscles aren't tense during your run.

Don't waste your speed.

Hesitation is a factor that can really hurt your speed. Keep your mind focused on running and don't worry about what will happen next. Sprinting runs can be helpful in opening up defenses and playing the ball at full speed.

Spend one workout per week doing speed training.

Focus on speed only during the workout, and give everything you have. Don't plan on anything stressful afterwards, but enjoy a day of lighter training and workouts.

Don't give up.

Keep your chin up even if you think nothing is happening. It takes time to build speed, and it can take weeks to improve by only a second. Don't get discouraged because you will definitely see you hard work pay off in your game.

Improve body strength.

Strength training is necessary for players who want to be stronger and last longer in the game. Try a cycle such as jogging for five minutes, then go into a run for five minutes, then slow back to a jog for five minutes. This is a great way to build strength and endurance.

74

Practice core stability training exercises.

Core strength training can be accomplished by doing sit-ups, crunches, and other core exercises. Many players try to mix it up a little by lifting their legs or other movements. This is good, but training stabilization exercises such as the plank are also necessary for strength training.

Use shorter sprints for fitness training.

It is not necessary for all training to be endurance training in soccer. Most of your runs are shorter runs on the field, therefore running five miles every day is not really the training you need. The same theory applies to strength training. It is better to lift more weight with fewer repetitions to build strength and become strong.

Get the Tip of the Week delivered straight to your inbox!

Head to
www.ArmChairGuides.com/PlayingSoccer

Sign up
for the **Playing Soccer: An Arm Chair Guide Full of 100 Tips to Getting Better at Soccer**
NEWSLETTER.

Join the Arm Chair Guides Newsletter and get a quick soccer tip each week for one whole year.

Train fast and heavy.

There are many methods for speed training. One of those is doing one fast and heavy day per week. For example, on Monday, you might run as quickly as you can while pulling a weighted sled behind you. Other days you might do speed training without the weight, or weight training without the speed factor.

Rest between repetitions.

It is important to rest between speed training repetitions. Speed training is not the same as fitness training, and requires that you are fresh and ready to go. If you are not resting enough between repetitions, your training can quickly become fitness training.

Train on one leg at a time.

Don't forget to train on one leg at a time. Most of the work done on the soccer field uses one leg at a time, even running. A single leg training regimen is necessary for balance and strength in each leg.

Master the technique.

Technique is an important factor to consider when strength training. For example, when doing body squats, start with little or no weight so that the technique is mastered first. It doesn't matter how many repetitions you do or how much weight you lift, if the technique is not right, no progress will be made.

Lessen the strain on the back.

Front squats can be done instead of back squats to relive stress on the back. You can lift fewer weights on front squats if your back gives your problems. Always remember technique is important in any exercise.

Correct excessive forward leaning.

If you notice excessive leaning during squats, there are some things to check. First of all, check to see if you're ankle has plenty of mobility. If you notice a lot of leaning, try placing a 2x4 under your heels. This may help keep your back straight and prevent leaning.

Get stronger and faster by lifting weights.

Lifting heavy weights promote intensity which will make you stronger and faster. These will then help you become a better soccer player.

Add some plyometric exercises.

Plyometrics are an important addition to your exercise routine that will give you speed and power. You can do this by starting with easy jumps and leaping up onto a box. Maintaining good technique is important. You don't have to jump over anything at first, but gradually increase your level of difficulty.

Move the ball quickly.

It is important to play the ball quickly in soccer to keep the opposing from getting back on defense or killing an attack. You should always be ready to receive a pass, and once you get the ball, go for it. Draw in a defender, and keep the flow of the game going by passing when your opponent is closing in.

85

Draw your leg back as if to shoot or pass.

You can freeze your defender by faking him or her out during play. Make them think you are about to take a long pass or shot by pulling your leg back like you're going to take a kick. This will freeze out your defender. Use your whole body especially shoulders and legs to sell the fake kick to your opponent.

Keep the ball moving.

It is important for the team to perform switch plays to throw off their defenders. Swing the ball from one side to other, and look for the area with the most space. Once you draw your opponents to one side of the field, throw the ball to a player on the other side when they start closing in. Keep the ball moving with one and two-touch soccer moves.

Perform a blind pass.

A quick switch, or blind pass, is a good way to catch the opposing team off guard and slip past them. You can do a quick switch by dribbling to the right, then swinging the ball to the left, and vice versa. The idea is that you are going in the direction you are dribbling, then switch to the opposite direction.

Cross the ball.

You can also fool your defenders by crossing the ball when you get it. Once they expect you to cross it, take the player on a dribble, then pass the ball to a teammate. Doing a cross may just open up the goal for a shot.

Play with better players.

It's always a good idea to challenge yourself when training for a soccer game. Try playing with older, more experienced players who have learned the tricks and skills of the game. You can learn a lot and become a better player by watching them and playing with them.

Let the ball do the work.

Sometimes it is necessary to slow down and allow the ball to do the work. You can't force the play, but just need to keep your mind moving and thinking. Young players must learn patience and sometimes it means just making an easy pass to an open player.

Think quickly.

As you progress in your level of play, you will have to learn to think quickly and make decisions. Shield the ball with your body while dribbling to keep defenders at bay. Look out for open players who may be able to get the ball to the goal. Get into the rhythm of the game, and quickly find the player with the best position to handle the ball.

Do a half-turn.

Players can do a half turn to see where other players are positioned in the field. Midfielders should be positioned to connect with forwards, while being half-turned to the sidelines. This gives you the optimal view of the back line, and intercept passes. Wing or touchline positions should be in a position that is open to the field.

Increase endurance using interval training.

Interval training is a mix of high intensity sprints with cardio workouts, and can be done for about an hour daily. Try starting at a normal speed for about 15 seconds, then doubling your speed for the next 15 seconds. You can also work intensely for one minute then slow down for a minute. This training will increase endurance on the field.

94

Switch it up between indoor and outdoor practice for full training.

In order to progress in your soccer skills, you must become focused on your practice drills. Practicing in an indoor space requires players to think fast and make better plays because of the confines of the walls.

95

Eat foods high in carbohydrates.

Carbohydrates provide the body with fuel for muscles to remain strong and healthy. They will also keep your energy level up and help you avoid fatigue. The American Dietetic Association recommends 3.6 grams daily for each pound of body weight you have. Carbs should be about 70% of your caloric intake.

96

Consume healthy carbs.

It is important to make sure you are eating healthy carbs such as whole-grain foods, as well as fruits and vegetables. Healthy carbs will not make your blood sugar spike and crash as simple carbs will do.

Add protein to your diet.

Protein should also be consumed for strength on the field. You should consume 0.6 to 0.8 grams of protein daily for every pound of body weight. Protein boosts the immune system and keeps you energized. Fish, poultry, low-fat dairy products, nuts, and soy are ideal proteins to consume.

98

Consume good fats but keep it low.

It may sound bad, but fats should also be a part of the soccer player's diet. There are definitely healthier choices for fatty foods, such as those that are heart-healthy, unsaturated fats, nuts, and foods made with olive oil. Players should eat about 0.45 grams of fat daily.

Maximize effectiveness by staying hydrated.

If you want to perform your best on the field, it is important that you stay hydrated. You should drink 2 cups of fluid before a game, and another during warm-ups. Two more cups should be consumed during half-time. Sports drinks with carbs and electrolytes may be chosen in place of water.

Recover properly.

Recovery time begins when the game ends. It is necessary for the body to recover for the next workout or game. Drink sports drinks, or consume 0.7 grams of carbs for every pound of body weight. Energy bars are also another option for getting carbs into your system to refuel your muscles.

Conclusion

This book may have given you some simple tips on how to improve your game and become a well-rounded player. But if you want to improve your skills whether it's shooting, passing, kicking, or running; practice is the only way to go. No matter the skill, there is always room for improvement. Kick the ball around on your own, or organize an impromptu game in the park with friends for practice. Having a natural talent is good but it's nothing without training and practice.

About Arm Chair Guides

Arm Chair Guides is a leading publisher of easy-to-read instructional and reference guides intended to help hobbyists just like us develop a better understanding of our passion through a series of short tips and advice.

Collected from across the globe via leading experts and topic authorities, each title consists of 100 tips focused on easily *implementable* ideas and techniques to help the hobbyist get the most from their pastime activities.

The perfect Christmas stocking stuffer, thank-you gift or *bedsider*, each Arm Chair Guide is designed to be a quick reference book that the reader can just pick up and flip through at their leisure.

To learn more about us and purchase our other titles, visit:
www.ArmChairGuides.com

Made in the USA
Lexington, KY
20 December 2011